EVERYDAY CALM

EVERYDAY CALM

Relaxing Rituals for Busy People

by **Darrin Zeer**
illustrations by **Cindy Luu**

CHRONICLE BOOKS
SAN FRANCISCO

Text copyright © 2003 by **Darrin Zeer.**
Illustrations copyright © 2003 by **Cindy Luu.**
All rights reserved. No part of this book may be reproduced
in any form without written permission from the publisher.

Library of Congress Cataloging-in-Publication Data available.

ISBN 0-8118-3757-2

Manufactured in China

Design by **Vanessa Dina**

Distributed in Canada by Raincoast Books
9050 Shaughnessy Street
Vancouver, BC V6P 6E5

10 9 8 7 6 5 4

Chronicle Books LLC
85 Second Street
San Francisco, California 94105

www.chroniclebooks.com

Find Calm

. . . within.

contents

QUICK HELP GUIDE

introduction

You're busy—who isn't these days? Whether at work or at play, you're always on the go. From the moment you wake up, as you drive through rush-hour traffic, when you're talking on your cell phone, until your head hits the pillow, you're in a hurry. And the drive to get things done is taking its toll. Your mind gets overwhelmed, and your body gets tense.

It's time to find calm. When you slow down and think clearly, you become more efficient. When you take time to be friendly and polite to those around you, the day is much more pleasant. When you're rested, you make fewer mistakes. When you take de-stress breaks, your creativity skyrockets. When you focus on giving to others, your relationships improve. Taking care of each area, step by step, you are guaranteed to find more peace of mind.

Everyday Calm has many quick tips and tricks for keeping your cool from morning to night. Learn how to get out of bed gracefully. Turn your home into a blissful sanctuary. Relax for a moment of meditation while you do the laundry. Make a "to do" list to manage your busy day, and try a yoga stretch while you wait in a long line. Slip into a cyber café for a virtual vacation. Indulge with a soothing soak in a scented bath. This book has relaxing ideas for your every need. Turn to the section that speaks to you: Tranquil Morning, Refreshing Midday, Effortless Afternoon, Easy Evening, Nurturing Nighttime—whichever part of your day needs a little calm.

To get started, open the book to any page and see what area of calm you discover. Or if you have a specific need, check out the Quick Help Guide on page 9. Whatever you do, if you make an effort to relax more during your day, I promise that you will find more fulfillment along the way. Take care, and enjoy yourself as you discover everyday calm.

five simple steps to
everyday calm

* 1 *

I will breathe and relax moment by moment.

* 2 *

I will stay calm and focused in all my interactions.

* 3 *

I will treat myself and others with care and patience.

* 4 *

If I feel overwhelmed I will take a calming break.

* 5 *

I will travel through my day peacefully.

tranquil
Morning

Start your day in a peaceful way.

wake-up Wisdom

Try to spend a calm moment before jumping out of bed and starting a busy day. Taking time to stretch will help you start your day on the right foot. In this exercise, focus on gently relaxing your mind and body.

1. Lie flat on your back and take a few breaths.

2. Notice any areas in your body that are sore or tense.

3. Gently raise your knees to your chest.

4. Wrap your arms around your knees and breathe deeply.

5. Let your knees slowly drop to one side.

6. Enjoy the stretch in your lower back and hips.

7. Take your time in the stretch; then switch sides.

8. When you're ready to get out of bed, slowly roll to your side and push yourself up with your hands.

yoga Yawn

Wake up, sleepyface! Here is a way to give yourself a natural face lift. Turn your morning yawning into a workout, to help relieve puffiness and stiff facial muscles. Yoga Yawns will enliven your face and mind.

1. Imagine that you are chewing an enormous piece of gum.

2. Move your mouth up and down, then side to side.

3. Stretch your face up and down while chewing.

✿ If you do this in your car or at your desk, expect some interesting reactions.

MOTIVATIONAL MIRROR SESSION

Stand strong and flex before your mirror. Fill your lungs with air. Shake your head or body if you just can't perk up. Give yourself a pep talk before launching into your day, and you'll receive an instant boost. For better or worse, this is the you you've got today! Check in to see how you are doing.

What is special about today? What challenges lie ahead? Any final words of encouragement? Try repeating this: "Today I will calmly conquer the world." Or make up a motivational phrase that is appropriate for you. Attach a note of your special reminder to the bathroom mirror.

Nothing great was ever achieved without enthusiasm.
—Ralph Waldo Emerson

INSTANT COFFEE BEND

This is a great stretch to do while you are waiting for the coffee to brew or the teakettle to boil. When you make room in your daily routine for a stretch, you'll be sure to feel the results all morning. When you finish the stretch, rise and enjoy your morning libation with renewed vigor.

1. Grab the counter edge and step back a couple of feet.

2. Spread your feet shoulder-width apart.

3. Let your upper body stretch down.

4. Enjoy the powerful stretch.

5. Try not to bob; your body is still waking up.

6. Relax your head and neck.

7. Focus on your breath to help loosen tightness.

8. When the coffeepot is full or the tea whistle blows, release out of the stretch.

I bend but do not break.
—Jean de La Fontaine

bar Hopping

Got the breakfast blahs? You know that you need to fill your belly to help you get up and go, so why not update your cereal or oatmeal with tasty toppings? Stock your pantry with these healthy treats and turn ho-hum basics into a new treat every day:

- ✿ **golden raisins**
- ✿ **shredded coconut**
- ✿ **fresh fruit**
- ✿ **carob chips**
- ✿ **nuts of all kinds**
- ✿ **plain or vanilla-flavored yogurt**
- ✿ **soy milk for a splash of protein**

 There is nothing either good or bad but thinking makes it so.

—Shakespeare

merry Morning mantras

While on the road or at home, take time to arouse your spirit. Chanting is a very powerful exercise. Buddhist monks can chant mantras for days at a time. Even a few minutes of chanting can help center you and release needless concerns. Try to develop your own mantras; tailor your chants to include good wishes for yourself and others.

"Ommm . . . let all my friends have a good day."
"Ommm . . . help me to stay calm in rush hour."

Focusing on a positive, nurturing phrase erases self-doubts. The "Om" is not an essential start but can be fun to add.

Instant a.m. Boosters

These quick and easy breathing exercises will jump-start your morning. If at any time you feel dizzy, simply stay seated and let your breathing return to normal.

INSTANT POWER

1. Find a comfortable place to sit down with your back straight and your shoulders relaxed.

2. Breathe in a deep, rapid motion through either just your nose or just your mouth, eight to ten times.

3. Pump your belly in with each exhale.

4. Take a moment to let your breathing return to normal before you stand up.

INSTANT ENERGY

1. Take a long breath in and hold it for eight counts. As you hold your breath, try to relax your body.

2. Exhale and hold your breath out for eight counts. Again, make sure you don't tense your muscles.

3. Let your facial muscles soften and relax. Drop your shoulders down.

Spa on the Go

There's nothing more refreshing than declaring a spa break whenever you need a little relaxation on the road. Let this stress-survival kit prepare you for every challenging situation. Be sure to start with a large bag that comfortably holds everything you'll need:

- ❀ A zippered pouch to hold spa items like anti-bacterial hand sanitizer, aloe hand lotion, lavender face spritzer, SPF 15 lip balm, and other special favorites.

- ❀ A bottle of water and healthful snacks like an energy bar or fruit.

- ❀ A selection of both relaxing and energizing music for your car and your portable player, to assist in mood elevation.

If you're the driver, leave an overnight bag in your car with dress and gym clothes, plus toiletries for unplanned workouts and spontaneous getaways.

Bag Archaeology

The more advanced society gets, the more stuff we seem to bring with us. During the day we need to carry our loads wisely, to avoid back or shoulder injuries. Make sure you carry only what you really need! Clear out those heavy extras and ancient layers of receipts and wrappers. Choose a bag that is easy to carry, with a cushioned strap. Practice keeping your back straight and your chest out, without leaning or slouching.

LOADING STRATEGY

1. When picking up bags, bend your knees and use your full-body strength.

2. Avoid reaching awkwardly for heavy bags.

3. When carrying loads, try to distribute the weight evenly on both sides; backpacks and messenger bags work best.

4. With shoulder bags, switch sides periodically.

5. Let your entire body get behind carrying the weight.

6. If one body part gets sore, shift the weight to the other side.

easy Efficient errands

When time is short and you have too many errands, make a plan. Write out a list, then mark the most urgent items with a star. Specify each location and map out the most efficient travel route. Search your mind for any forgotten items. Once the list is complete, get into action. Check in with friends and neighbors for a round of errand swapping. Can you pick up a neighbor's dry cleaning while she returns your movies? Be prepared for pleasant surprises and unplanned pitfalls. Keep a quick pace, letting tension slide away as each errand is completed. Stay focused. Don't be surprised if you finish the job in record time, thanks to the magic of Easy Efficient Errands.

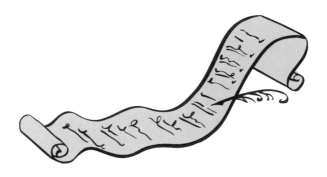

DOORWAY DISCIPLINE

Before you touch that doorknob, avoid unwanted stress by making sure all important items are packed with you. Taking this extra minute may save you hours later. Before stepping into the vast unknown, go through this final checklist:

1. Have I got my keys, watch, wallet, and cash?
2. Do I know how to get where I am going?
3. Do I need to mail any letters or return library books?
4. One last look to make sure all is in order.

Take a breath, step out, and have a great day . . .

 He who is in a hurry rides on a donkey.
—German proverb

WISDOM OF THE HORN

Attention all road warriors: Put your temper in cruise control! Rush hour can be one of the greatest challenges of the day. The primal desire to hit your horn is always inviting. But don't let the stress ruin your day. Become a master of your emotions:

- ✿ If there is no danger, stay off the horn.

- ✿ Take a breath, scream, or yell if you like.

- ✿ Forget those rhapsodies of roadside revenge.

- ✿ Practice letting go of the overwhelming tension.

- ✿ Imagine that the driver in front of you is a close friend.

- ✿ For the advanced commuter: Try smiling and waving to nearby motorists.

CHAIR Karma

Tension can rise as you race toward work on the train or bus. One way to step out of the morning commuter funk is by performing a random act of giving. When you see someone in need, rise to the occasion and offer your seat. Don't take no for an answer. Notice the rush of good feeling that comes upon you. Don't be shy as fellow commuters shower you with good vibrations and warm wishes.

 A man's true wealth is the good he does in this world.
—Muhammad

refreshing
Midday

Take a break and feel renewed.

TWO-MINUTE MIDDAY CALM

If you find yourself lacking calmness and clarity, take a two-minute break to de-stress. Stop what you're doing, turn the phones off, and sit quietly. For two minutes you will do nothing but breathe and relax. Your mind will be chattering, but tell it to be quiet. Keep returning to your deep, relaxing breaths. Each time you get caught in busy thoughts, return to your breathing. Your muscles may feel tight, so let the breathing help relax your body. When the two minutes are complete, notice your state. As you return to your day, go slowly and use this calm that you found as a tool for efficiency. You may get sudden realizations or remember forgotten appointments; take time to write them down. Whenever you feel overwhelmed, try this quick fix; don't forget how easy it is to feel so good.

Revolving-Door Policy

Time-tested etiquette will never be out of style, and being
a gentleman or gentlewoman will get you everywhere.
Next time you find yourself in front of a doorway, open
it and let oncoming traffic through. Opening a door for
another person is one simple way to offer support. (To
become a master door opener, pay attention to bellmen
at fancy hotels.) Just follow these easy steps:

1. Announce "After you" to those passing by.
2. Open the door wide, step back, and remember to smile.
3. Look back and see if anyone else may need your service.

The twinkling eyes of gratitude will be ample repayment.
While you may have made someone else's day, you have
also undoubtedly improved yours!

PICNIC Paradise

Add some green to your day! You can wash your troubles away by simply immersing yourself in a park. Take a walk or just sit for a while. Staring at lush greenery can ease eyestrain from computer monitors and fluorescent lights and help provide a sense of general well-being. A nap in a park can be deeply resuscitating. Arrange a healthful picnic snack for your lunch hour. Surprise a workmate or friend for lunch with a twist. Be patient and let nature do its thing. Treat yourself to simple pleasures. A calm and peaceful break will alter your day for the better.

TROPICAL URBAN OASIS

Slip out of your day and have a tropical fruit juice fix.
When you are squeezed for time, juice shops offer a meal
in a cup and an upbeat atmosphere. Add all the extras for
a much-needed energy boost. For smoothies, ask for
real yogurt rather than frozen yogurt. If you are feeling
adventurous, order one or two shots of wheatgrass juice.
As a chaser, order a carrot-and-orange-juice mix. Make
sure you sit down for this one, as you may feel a slight
body jolt. Wheatgrass packs a punch with a megadose of
vitamin C and a long list of nutrients to help detoxify and
recharge the body.

CYBER Café HOLIDAY

Ready to transport yourself into a dream virtual vacation?
Take time out from a busy day of shopping or errands.
Armed with a drink and a snack, book a trip into cyber-
space on an imaginary holiday.

1. Sit down and search for your dream destina-
   tions—perhaps Thailand, Maui, or Paris.

2. As each site downloads, drop your head and
   feel your neck relax. Slowly roll your head in
   circles.

3. Now let the Web site transport you to Hawaii
   or your own idea of paradise.

✿ If your fingers are tight from tapping the keys,
   squeeze them into a firm animal claw. Then
   make fists and roll your hands in wide circles,
   both directions.

Relax on your online beach blanket!

Wherever I go, there I am.
—Aristotle

cleansing Cleaning

Pent-up frustration can be used for positive results. Dust off your cleaning equipment and get scrubbing. As you transform your household, you'll also wash away internal anxiety. Your floors will shine as your mind unwinds. Dig into corners. Turn up the good old rock 'n' roll and dance while you work. You can't clean everything, so don't worry about finishing; just keep going as long as you enjoy it. Find contentment in the activity and stay in the moment. Who would have thought cleaning could be so enriching?

TAKE a GRAVITY BREAK

The mind and body are intimately connected. If you notice yourself getting tired and cranky, take a break to think about your body. Most likely your spine will have begun to slump down. By simply standing straight and consciously breathing, you can make a quick mood shift. Over time, poor posture and a tense mind create unnecessary aches and pains. Stay positive and healthy with these easy steps:

1. **Keep your chest out with chin tucked down slightly.**

2. **Pull your shoulders back and down.**

3. **Feel your feet firmly planted on the ground.**

4. **Let your face soften and relax.**

5. **Relax your belly and rhythmically breathe slowly and deeply.**

Your mood will elevate as your posture rises up!

COMMUNITY Calm

Potential serenity busters abound in subways, elevators, restaurants, stores, and even movie theaters. Noise and crowds get to all of us. Train yourself to overlook the small stuff. Commit yourself to relaxing and enjoying yourself in spite of the mishaps. Your calm attitude will help turn your day into a hit, and your relaxed manner is sure to rub off on everyone around you!

 I have noticed that folks are generally about as happy as they make up their minds to be.

—Abraham Lincoln

A LITTLE TASTE OF HEAVEN

Sanctuary, serenity, peace, and spirituality are always close at hand. Take a step into a church, synagogue, or mosque and spend some quiet time. Find calmness and clarity as you travel within.

1. Turn off your phone or pager as you embark on this mini-retreat.

2. Before going inside, center yourself with a few calm breaths.

3. Enter the building and quietly find a seat.

4. Close your eyes and let your body relax.

5. Allow the sacred space to envelop you in calm.

6. Focus on what's important in your life.

7. Ask, how can you put your heart's desire into action?

Notice how thoughts of gratitude will suddenly arise!

effortless
Afternoon

Keep your cool the whole day through.

karaoke on the Go

Here is a great way to perk up from the afternoon blahs. Whistle while you walk or drive, or anywhere where you know it won't bother those around you. Let spontaneity reach its greatest heights. Sing your theme song or your favorite commercial. When you sing a tune, all your troubles melt away. Sing from your belly, and don't hold anything back. Your tension will instantly change into a smile.

 There is no great genius without some touch of madness.
—Lucius Annaeus Seneca

urban Obstacle course

Daydreamers beware! Multitasking is a tempting time-saver that can be hazardous to your health. Sidewalks can be cluttered with obstacles, and you've got to be careful near busy streets. The challenge is to arrive at your destination safely. As you go about your business, walking, talking, and contemplating, keep a keen eye on what's ahead of you. Anticipate possible roadblocks. Beware especially when talking on your cell phone or immersed in conversation. Staying sharp and alert will help guide you safely around town.

Experience is the name everyone gives to their mistakes.

—Oscar Wilde

caLL-Drop desperaTION

Cell-phone reception can disappear at the most inopportune moments. As with any frustrating technological malfunction, it's important to get a grip on the emotional downturn that follows. Take a breath, have a laugh, and then redial. Sometimes a break in a call is just what you need to refocus and adjust your position.

Here is a quick stretch fix for when calls get dropped:

1. **Inhale deeply through your nose.**

2. **Shrug your shoulders to your ears and hold for a moment.**

3. **Exhale thoroughly and let your shoulders drop.**

the Great escape

Make your car a sanctuary, a place to find solitude away from home. Keep the car stocked with snacks, bottled water, and a selection of relaxing music to help you wind down. Parked on the side of a street or in a parking lot, let the music play, recline your seat, close your eyes, and take five. Steal moments for yourself in the midst of the every-day chaos. Notice how calm and efficient you become with each rest stop. This is your own private hideaway.

After a storm comes a calm.
—Matthew Henry

AFTER-WORK
WINDOW GAZING

Take window-shopping to another level. After work, go for a stroll down your town's main street. Let your mind unwind and soak up the sights and sounds of the neighborhood. Step by step, relax and breathe. To disengage your mind from work, notice the latest styles and colors in each shop window. Let the sights and sounds soothe your tension. Accomplish nothing but walking and window gazing. By the time you return home, you will be feeling renewed and ready for friends and family.

DRAWER DHARMA

The teachings of Buddha are often referred to as the dharma, a term that can be translated as "truth." The state of your desk or drawers reveals certain truths about your life. You can't be calm if your surroundings reflect chaos. Inner order relies on every item being in its perfect place.

1. Open a drawer and see what's inside.

2. Take out any items you don't need and give them away.

3. Place each item for ease of use.

4. Use containers to organize the small stuff.

5. Notice how your drawer and your mind fall into order simultaneously.

✿ Your goal is to keep all areas of your life in order, so one at a time, tackle all the drawers in your home.

By the work one knows the workman.

—Jean de La Fontaine

TUMBLE-DRY
MEDITATION

When you're in a hurry and your clothes just won't dry, it's easy to let impatience get the best of you. Instead, make the most of the time you have.

1. Pull up a chair in front of the dryer and get comfortable.

2. Close your eyes and focus on the tumbling of your clothes.

3. Let the rhythmic sound calm your mind.

4. Breathe in unison to each circling motion.

5. Imagine that you are at the beach, with the waves crashing ashore.

6. When buzzer sounds, end your meditation session.

7. Pull on your toasty warm clothes in comfort and serenity.

saturday Saints

The week is short, and you have so much to do. For a new perspective, take the time to volunteer on a Saturday afternoon. Pick a Saturday to give half a day to others and you'll feel fulfilled all week long. Make a date of it by bringing along friends and family. Search the Internet or the phone book to find the organization of your choice. And if you can't spare time, share your money and expertise. All of us have so much to offer.

 I cried because I had no shoes until I met a man who had no feet.

—Persian saying

reinCARnation

Caught in a parking-lot maze? Wondering where you parked your car? At first, the rows of seemingly identical vehicles can be overwhelming. Turn this moment into a walking meditation. Forget your hurry and bring your thoughts into focus. Take a deep breath and discover your car. Your car is waiting patiently for your return. Take time and enjoy the search!

 Self-trust is the first secret of success.
—Ralph Waldo Emerson

DOG TRAINING

When tension takes over, time spent with your faithful furry companion is a lesson in the good things in life. Let your animal instinct take over and unleash some fun. Your pets will teach *you* a few new tricks:

- ✿ Use baby talk in public without fear of strange stares.

- ✿ Take daily walking excursions to parks, mountains, and beaches.

- ✿ Cuddle unabashedly.

- ✿ Receive unannounced wet slobbering licks on feet or face without a care.

- ✿ Take precious care of another living being.

- ✿ Create immediate good chemistry with all passersby.

 Great is the man who has not lost his childlike heart.
—Mencius

easy
Evening

Unwind with friends and fun.

THE CINEMA STRETCH

Almost everyone loves the movies, but the rush to get to
the cinema on time, wait in line for tickets, and find a
seat can take its toll. Try this quick stretch for your hips
to relax your muscles before the film starts and help you
sit comfortably until the credits roll.

1. Cross your legs, placing your right ankle
   above your left knee.

2. Gently push your right knee down, so that you
   feel a stretch in your right hip. Take your time
   in the stretch, relaxing your hip and buttocks.

3. Switch legs and repeat the stretch on the
   other side.

WORKOUT WISDOM

Working out can be blissful or a chore, depending on
your state of mind. As you strain to bench-press the
barbell, notice whether your mind is also weighed down.
Clear your head, and your physical load will lighten, too.
Tap into your enthusiasm and let your workout be easy.
Whenever you feel drained, coach yourself compassion-
ately, like an internal personal trainer. Take deep breaths
on each repetition and, to avoid injury, lift with your
entire body strength. This is your private time to go
within. A deep peace will follow. Savor that feeling by
recuperating with some stretching and sauna or steam
afterward. Use this positive boost to motor through the
rest of your day.

Strong body, strong mind, strong desire!

cab Charisma

Taxi drivers can pop into our lives from around any street corner. Many offer more than transportation; they lend an ear. Taxicab confessions can provide a warm encounter with a stranger. Don't be afraid to ask for information about the latest restaurants and attractions; most drivers know their way around town and are more than willing to share their wisdom. Many drivers are excellent listeners and would love to hear your tales. Sit back and rest, and trust your driver to navigate through the city.

groove Therapy

A little bump and boogie can recharge your body and mind. The more uninhibited you are, the more relaxed you'll be. You can always put on the stereo at home, but dancing at a club or party with lots of people can inspire you to greater heights. If you feel self-conscious, follow this groovy six-step guide:

1. Get up and dance; a partner is nice, but not essential.

2. Find a spot on the floor with a little elbow room.

3. Drop the old steps and explore different rhythms.

4. Get out of your mind and into your body.

5. Take deep breaths and stretch while you dance.

6. Feel the freedom and get inspired.

 Minds are like parachutes. They only function when they are open.

—Sir James Dewar

LINE-UP LOOSENING

Stuck standing in line for a concert, sports event, or movie? Feel like the wait is eternal? This Line-up Loosening routine will set you at ease.

1. Place your hands on your waist and do circles with your hips.

2. Place your hands on your buttocks, fingers pointing down, and stretch your upper body slowly back. Keep your feet firmly planted on the ground for balance.

If you are waiting with friends, try a Line-up Loosening massage:

1. Ask permission to massage their shoulders.

2. Stand behind the willing person and place your hands on their shoulders.

3. Squeeze their neck and shoulder muscles slowly and firmly.

Victory belongs to the most persevering.

—Napoleon

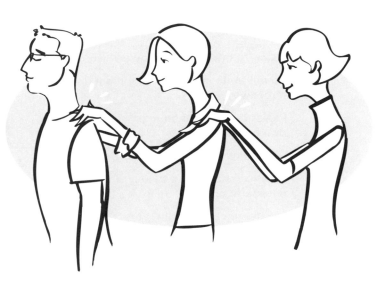

PERSONALITY POINTERS

When a friend or stranger erupts into a grown-up version of a temper tantrum, it's time to pause and offer assistance. All of us can blow up with frustration, given the wrong set of circumstances. Keep these principles in place for the sake of harmony:

1. Listen to the tantrum thrower's words.

2. Do not try to cut off or calm them down right away.

3. Resist the temptation to join in with your own tantrum.

4. Don't take any accusations personally.

5. Breathe, relax, and patiently wait for the release to end.

6. Ask if you can offer the person assistance.

Most tantrum throwers just need to get it out and will settle down on their own. Sometimes just being there is enough to help someone else get through their struggles.

Anger is a short madness.

—Horace

LISTENING TO
Body language

Become bilingual in minutes by learning to read body language. If you are interacting with someone whose body is twisted up like a pretzel, it is likely that any further communication will prove futile. Attempt to counteract the situation by relaxing and hanging loose; wait for an opening. Master the art of observation with some simple body-language lessons.

ARMS AND LEGS:

1. If arms and legs are crossed, you should withdraw forceful questions and focus on being friendly.

2. If arms and/or legs are loose and relaxed, proceed without concern.

FACE AND EYES:

1. If eyes are looking upward, the listener is considering something.

2. If eyes are darting around, the listener may feel threatened or uncomfortable.

3. Tense facial muscles may be a sign that the listener is suffering information overload and it's time to take a break.

BLISS ON Aisle 6

Caffeine and sugar-laden foods seem like great quick
fixes for stress, but if your body is loaded with stimulants,
you'll actually increase your chances of being agitated.
On your next supermarket trip, open yourself up to the
healthy zone. Slow down in the produce aisle to see if you
can discover ways to satisfy your munchies with fresh,
healthful foods. Explore different fruits and vegetables
you've never tried before. Plan a spontaneous soup or
salad. Collect different kinds of nuts and raisins for an
on-the-go power mix. Herbal teas are an interesting and
exotic switch from coffee. Are you weary? When you've
filled your cart with healthful snacks, cool down in the
freezer section with an all-natural fruit pop.

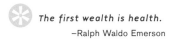 *The first wealth is health.*
–Ralph Waldo Emerson

PRImaL TheRaPy

Watching the game at a favorite bar is a tribal tradition. Gather the gang together! Get rowdy and unwind by cheering for the home team. Let it out after a long week in the trenches, and don't be afraid to stretch your vocal cords. Decompress. Get connected to your primal energy. When your team scores, bellow out ape sounds from deep in your belly—"Hooh, hooh, hooh, hooh!"—as you pump your fist in the air.

On the day of victory no one is tired.
—Arab proverb

Restaurant Feng shui

Just as you pick a restaurant that matches your mood, make sure that you're seated at a table that sets the right tone for your meal. It's worth waiting for. Feng shui is the art of harmonious placement, and it can apply to where you sit. When entering a restaurant, choose a table with comfortable chairs, a nice view, and a soothing atmosphere. Try to distance yourself from the heavy-traffic areas. Create a pleasant environment by developing a friendly rapport with your server. Before you eat, give thanks and gratitude for the food and companionship! Make a silent affirmation that this meal will be peaceful and that you will enjoy some good company. Taking your time and staying conscious of your experience is sure to turn a quick bite into a meal to be remembered.

nurturing
Nighttime

End the day as peacefully as it began.

DELIGHTFUL DELIVERY

Comfort food with spice can be very nice!

When you want a unique dining experience but are too tired to leave the house, break out the fine china and order in. Indian or Thai food can be a treat. Request a mild sauce for a fiery yet stomach-soothing experience. Set up a getaway space on your living room floor. The comforts of home combined with exotic aromas are sure to send you on a mental holiday. Candles and calming music make the setting complete!

 Take rest; a field that has rested gives a bountiful crop.

—Ovid

INSTANT P.M. MELLOW

These two anytime, anywhere gentle breathing exercises are great escapes from your hectic schedule. Before you begin, find a comfortable place to sit down and let go of your busy day.

INSTANT CALM:

1. Inhale deeply and slowly, counting as you breathe in.

2. Count as you exhale and make the out breath twice as long as the in breath was.

3. Don't worry about how high you count; just focus on relaxing your entire body.

INSTANT PEACE:

1. Using your right thumb, cover the right nostril and inhale through your left nostril.

2. Place your index finger over the left nostril and exhale through your right nostril.

3. Go slowly and focus on relaxing your thoughts.

4. Repeat for eight to ten breaths, or until you feel relaxed.

journal Therapy

After you have completed your business for the day, step out of work mode and into a more relaxed state. The main idea behind writing in your journal is to help you open up to your feelings and cast aside your worries. Pent-up emotion creates tension and confusion. After a busy day, writing down your thoughts can help you unwind and prepare for a peaceful sleep. Try setting an egg timer for five minutes and writing whatever pops into your head in that time. Soon you'll find it interesting to look over your notes from the past weeks and months and see how you are changing for the better and gaining new perspectives. What you were once so worried about is now forgotten! To be a successful journal writer, be as honest as you can on paper. By opening up, you will feel a deeper under-standing of yourself and a greater ability to handle your daily challenges.

Happiness does not consist of having what you want, but wanting what you have.

–Confucius

LOUNGER Levitation

During commercial breaks in your favorite TV show or the Big Game, hit the mute button, sit back, get comfortable, and close your eyes. Let your body levitate in your recliner, couch, or bed. Visualize your body completely limp. Take deep, long relaxing breaths. With each exhalation, allow the day's stresses to melt away. Do a body scan, starting from your head and moving slowly down, relaxing your body part by part. Imagine that you are floating on a cloud in your living room. Take a rest; the world will wait patiently for your return.

 The hardest work of all is to do nothing.

—Proverb

closet Catwalk

Take a break from your couture savvy! Go on an adventure
into your closet in search of something different to wear
around the house. Relieve yourself of fashion sense and
mix and match spontaneously. Dress up your divine self.
By wearing different colors and outfits, you can inspire a
deep inner creativity. Don't fret—you don't have to go out
in public; this is purely for you to enjoy! A little freedom
from style can help you unwind and get more comfortable
after a long day. You may make new style discoveries and
want to change your entire wardrobe. But if you don't, at
least no one saw you!

Beauty is in the eye of the beholder.
—Margaret Wolfe Hungerford

RUB-A-DUB Yoga
IN THE TUB

Take a step into the relaxation zone! Schedule a meeting just for you, your bath salts, and your bathtub. Add a few drops of lavender essential oil for a relaxing aromatic touch. Dim the lights, light the candles, and stop the action. Focus on melting tension away.

Help your muscles relax in the warm water by trying this stretch.

1. While sitting in the tub, brace your hands underneath your calves.

2. Place the soles of your feet flat against the end of the bathtub.

3. Gently lower your upper body into a forward bend.

4. Let your head drop forward and relax your neck muscles.

5. Breathe and relax into the stretch.

Be patient with yourself; peace and relaxation will arrive.

SLEEP SERENITY

Even when you're tired it can be hard to fall asleep. This exercise is sure to bring on the Z's. Get into bed and lie flat on your back with your arms and legs apart. Take long and deep breaths, imagining that you are breathing into your whole body. After taking a deep inhalation, hold your breath. Practice tightening all the muscles in your body and hold tight for a few moments. Exhale and release all your muscles, imagining that each muscle is limp and relaxed. Repeat this practice three times, or until you can feel your body melting into your mattress. This will help you fall asleep peacefully.

What we think, we become.

—Buddha

BIOGRAPHIES

Darrin Zeer, a self-styled relaxation consultant, is also the author of *Office Yoga* and *Office Spa*, both from Chronicle Books. He travels around North America encouraging people to stay calm, enjoy their work, and be successful. He has appeared on CNN, in *Time* magazine, on NPR radio, on Web MD, and in hundreds of other media venues. Darrin spent seven years in Asia studying the Eastern arts of healing and meditation. He lives in Hawaii and California, where he writes and also consults for companies like 3M, Four Seasons Resort, and Glen Ivy Hot Springs Spa. Darrin is involved in the Miracle of Love Intensive, a six-day spiritual program that is offered in many cities around the world. If you or your company would like to contact the author, please visit his Web site at **www.relaxationconsultants.com.**

Cindy Luu is a New York City–based illustrator and graphic designer whose clients include Bloomingdale's and Ann Taylor. She is a graduate of the Rhode Island School of Design. This is her first book.

acknowledgments

Special special thanks to Kalindi for being my inspiration! Thanks also to my wife, Monique; my parents, Louis and Carole; my editor, Lisa Campbell; my agent, Jeffrey Herman; my mentor, John Mapleback; and editor John Pine and publicist Debbie Matsumoto. Also to Damien, Lara, Scotti, Ginny, Blaze, Marcus, Siegmar, Kris, G'Angela, Hans, Deb, Christoph, Alison, Savanna, Faith, Robert, David, Dave K., Gina, and all my family and friends around the globe. I couldn't have done it without you!

 To truly live and become aware takes great courage.

—Gourasana

 We do not see things as they are.
We see things as we are.

—Talmud